MW01289372

THE RIDE
OF
YOUR LIFE

The Incredible Journey
of Following Jesus

By
Bobby Martin

TABLE OF CONTENTS

A Note to Readers

The following chapters are a result of countless hours of studying the Biblical invitations of Jesus to follow Him as well as years of experience in my personal journey of following Christ. I encourage the reader to read each of the Scriptural accounts that are alluded to in each chapter and to let God speak to you in a personal way as He has to me. Your journey will not look like mine, but the principles are very much the same. My hope and prayer for all is that wherever you are in the journey – beginning, middle, or end – that these words will encourage you to continue the ride of your life.

CHAPTER 1

Let's Ride

*"My sheep listen to my voice; I know
them, and they follow me"*

John 10:27 (TNIV)

It was 1978, and I was about to graduate from high school and start college life. There was no internet back then and there were certainly no smart phones. However, electronics had come a long way and had joined the toy industry to produce some great games. It was that year, 1978, when Milton Bradley came out with an electronic game called "Simon". The device had four colored buttons, each producing a particular tone when it was pressed. A round in the game consisted of the lighting up of one or more buttons in a random order, after which the player must reproduce that order by pressing the buttons. With each success came a faster pattern. The game really took off and became a pop culture icon in the 1980's.

The Simon game inspired many imitators and knockoffs such as "Pocket Repeat" and "Copy Cat". We college kids could only afford the knockoffs, so "Copy Cat" became the craze between classes. You could hear the definite tones and patterns ringing throughout the dorm rooms. I'm sure the game improved memory and motor skills, but one thing was bound to happen. The pattern became so complicated and so fast, you would eventually fail.

For a long time my approach to Christianity resembled that "Copy Cat" game. I wasn't trying to imitate colors, sounds, and patterns. I was attempting to play "Copy Jesus". I tried to pray like Jesus, act like Jesus, and live like Jesus. My attempts would take off strong, but before long I would sputter. Early on I learned that it was very difficult to stay in the game. You get out and feel guilty for failing. You try to start over, but it's like you know at some point you are going to fail again.

One problem with "Copy Jesus" was I did get out a lot. Not only that, but I somewhat learned to like getting out. If you got out you didn't have to play anymore. It was a very difficult game to play, much less win. Who could do everything like Jesus did? When I sinned and got out of the game, I decided I would spend some time sinning because I was out anyway. Then I would hear a very convicting sermon or read an inspiring book, get back in the game and try again.

Another problem with "Copy Jesus" was seeing people who were extremely good at the game. They could pray like Jesus, act like Jesus, love like Jesus, forgive like Jesus, and live like Jesus. They were so consistent and I concluded I would never be able to stay in the game as long as they did. Somehow, they had learned the secret to playing the game and winning.

Still another problem was people I knew who had never played the game. They certainly weren't Christ followers and I thought they needed to play "Copy Jesus". It seemed they had no guilt and could do whatever they wanted. Even though they were not playing, part of me was somewhat envious of them. But someone would tell me that I needed to get those people into the game, even though I was not very good at the game. Who am I to tell anybody to get in this game that almost no one seemed to win?

Maybe that's how Christianity was presented to you.

Follow the patterns - become a Christian, pray a prayer, sign a card, and join the church. Afterwards you get into this life long game of copying Jesus. You tried that for a while and not only were you not any good at it; you didn't even want to play. There wasn't any joy in it and the people you saw play it consistently were people you didn't want to be like anyway. What was the point of playing?

Thankfully, I have learned that Christianity is not a game of copying Jesus or God or anybody for that matter. The essence of the Christian life is a relationship between very imperfect human beings and a very perfect God. The reason Jesus came to this earth was because the whole religious world was in this endless, monotonous game of copycat. You must copy God or you will lose. The law, the Ten Commandments, the sacrificial system - all were patterns to imitate and if you failed you were out of the game. Everybody was trying but they were losing the game. Consequently, Jesus came to say this wasn't a game of copying Him. It was supposed to be a love relationship. If you forget or don't know that, you gravite toward the game whether you are a religious person or not. You discover you're not very good at it, and you sit out until you are convicted to get back in. The cycle is endless.

Jesus did not come to give us more patterns to repeat or things to do and not do. If that had been the case Jesus would have offered us a list. But He didn't come with a list, and that's what frustrated all the religious leaders. They had "the list" for years and had made it into a game. They weren't any good at is so they kept changing the rules so they could stay in the game. The fact was they had been out of the game a long time because nobody is that good.

It would be like approaching marriage with the goal of copying the perfect marriage. You make a list of patterns to copy: Say the perfect words, tell her that dress is pretty, make a big deal about her hair, go shopping with her, etc.

What if our whole focus was on keeping the rules and trying to imitate what we are told are the perfect patterns of marriage? What type of relationship would that be? You may be approaching marriage like that and it's not working for you. It may have started as a loving relationship but it has devolved into trying to be a good spouse and trying to say and do the right things. *"I'm committed to marriage,"* you would say. There is nothing worse than being committed to marriage. I don't want my wife to be committed to marriage. I want her to be committed to me.

That analogy occurs for many of us who fell in love with Jesus. We forget about the relationship and become committed to Christianity. We turn into believers who care more about being religious and doing the right things. It progresses into a game again of copying Jesus instead of loving Jesus. God sent Jesus into the world to blast the myth of that entire system. He wants you to have a relationship with Him and it is completely different than playing a game. When Jesus was on earth He talked about this relationship in different ways. At times He said it resembled a shepherd and sheep. At times he said it was like a father and child. On one occasion He compared it to a vine and a branch. Every image He used was very relational. It was, and always has been, about a relationship.

It is interesting the game "Copy Cat" was later repackaged by Sears under the name "Follow Me". Consequently, those are the words that Jesus used when he invited someone into a relationship. Yet when Jesus says the words *"Follow Me"* it is never meant to be a game. Instead, it's a very simple two word picture that is easy for me to connect with every single day. It calls me away from the copycat mentality and back toward a relationship with God. It is an invitation to take a ride on the journey of a lifetime, or what I would call "the ride of your life".

The invitation to ride is an invitation to follow Jesus.

Jesus says, *"Let's ride!"* and He invites us to follow Him on this ride. As we will see later, not everyone accepts the invitation. But many do and many have. In the chapters ahead we will discover what the ride looks like, and what happened when people accepted his invitation to follow Him. Are you ready? Let's ride!

CHAPTER 2

No Toll Booths

*"'Follow me,' he told him, and Matthew
got up and followed him."*

Matthew 9:9b (TNIV)

Some may have called it a mid-life crisis, but a few years ago I acquired a motorcycle. When I walked into the Harley Davidson dealership, I had never ridden a motorcycle in my life. The sales person was extremely understanding and gently guided me through the steps of purchasing my first ride. After selecting the bike, I was led to the helmet section to pick out a helmet. Everyone was courteous and friendly. They introduced me to the people in the service department as well as the parts department, all of them very congenial. The entire buying experience was such a pleasant one. What I will never forget was when I signed the paperwork and the purchase was finalized, everyone in the store said, *"Welcome to the family."* I learned that day that Harley Davidson buyers and riders were like a community.

Some time later, however, I discovered that bikers in general had a stereotype. I experienced this one summer when a friend of mine and I wrote our motorcycles up to Church Camp to see our kids. We drove into the encampment and stopped near where we thought the kids were staying. Of course, we had our "biker" clothes on, dew rags and all. A moment later a vehicle stopped by and man inside informed us we had to "check in". I had been to this camp many times and never had to check in. I'm a pastor for goodness sake. It was then I learned that some "church people" draw quick conclusions about bikers, practically putting them into a category of their own.

When Jesus uses the words "Follow Me" for the very first time, He uses them to issue the invitation to an individual no one would ever dream of asking to come along for the ride. His name was Matthew and he was a tax collector. People hated tax collectors. They were put into a category of their own. There were sinners, and there were tax collectors. These guys were even excluded from the religious activities. They were barred from the temple, excluded from making sacrifices, and were not allowed to participate in the religious festivals.

Back in those days you actually purchased the right to be a tax collector. You went to the Roman government and you bid on the job and the highest bidder was granted the opportunity to collect taxes. As a chief tax collector, you could hire additional people to work for you, and you were given a region for which you were responsible for collecting a certain amount of money. Anything you added to that amount was completely your business. You could add a surcharge to the taxes and that's how you paid yourself. As a result tax collectors were hated by the Jewish people because they were being cheated by their own countrymen.

There were all kinds of taxes – bridge taxes, border taxes, export and import taxes, fruit taxes, wine taxes – it went on and on. There was no rhyme or reason to the system. They would set up these booths anywhere they wanted and collect taxes to make sure Rome got its money. It is easy to see why these men were considered a notch lower than sinners. Jesus, however, had a different view.

One day Jesus and his group were traveling and they

came upon one of these tax booths. It might have been a bridge, a border, or maybe a city. But suddenly there was one of these tax booths you walked by and you had to pay your taxes. Jesus approaches the booth and sitting there is Matthew. Matthew was possibly someone who worked for one of the chief tax collectors. He has bought into this system of taxing his own countrymen. Jesus comes up to him and says, *"Follow Me"*. For the group with Jesus, that's the last thing they would expect Jesus to say to a tax collector. Instead, they would expect Him to tell Matthew to clean up his act, or repent and stop being a traitor to his country. There are many things you would assume Jesus to say to Matthew, a tax collector. Yet Jesus says *"Matthew, follow Me"*.

The thoughts of those who were with Jesus that day were probably predictable. *"You want him to be with us?" I can see why You want us to follow You. But You want us to associate with him? Don't You get it, Jesus? He's a TAX COLLECTOR, for heaven's sake."* They did not understand an important truth. **The invitation to follow Jesus is for sinners**. Even if you are not a religious person this invitation is extended to you. Or you may have been a Christian for years and somewhere along the way you decided you had enough. You went through a difficult time such as a divorce, a death, or some other tragedy that caused you to lose faith in God. Maybe you are trying to reconnect now. If so, this invitation is for you.

Perhaps you are wondering if God will take you back. You understand why He took Matthew. He didn't know any better. But you grew up in the church and turned your back on God. Why would Jesus want to associate with you? I have good news. This invitation is extended to you. The invitation to follow Jesus is an invitation to sinners. If you're not a sinner you don't need to follow Jesus because you don't need Jesus. However, the great thing about this is we are all on common ground. Every day, wherever we are and whatever we know, Jesus invites us to follow Him and get in on the ride of our lives.

Jesus invites this tax collector, this sinner in a category of his own, to follow Him. Matthew does an unusual thing. He stands up and follows Jesus. There were a lot of things Jesus could have asked Matthew to do that day that he would not have done. He could have asked him to follow and be a martyr. He could have asked him to leave his possessions and family to follow. If Jesus had asked Matthew to do something like that it is likely he would have refused. But Jesus, because he knew where Matthew was, asked him to do something he was able to do. There was no "to do" list and there were no change orders. An invitation to follow Jesus was the only thing offered. The Bible says Matthew got up and did what Jesus asked him to do.

Here's why I like this story and why we are going to look at following Jesus for the next few chapters. That invitation has been extended to all of us. In fact, Jesus extends it to us every single day of our lives. It's been offered to every human being since the time Jesus first proposed it to Matthew. Please understand it is not an invitation to clean up your act nor is it an invitation to make a lot of changes. This is not a request to stop doing this or start doing that. It is an invitation that is extended to us where we are at this moment. Jesus simply invites us to follow Him. I love that because I don't have to worry about how well am I doing in the game. It is not necessary to concern myself about how I am doing compared to everyone else. The only question I need to ask every morning is a simple one: Am I following Jesus?

There were some additional people watching this entire encounter and they were very disturbed by what happened. Some of Jesus' own followers were concerned by this. However, there were some Pharisees, the religious leaders of the day, who saw this whole thing. A lot of thoughts are going through their minds. *"Jesus, how can you ask somebody who has no holiness, no religion, no righteousness, no good deeds to follow you? Shouldn't there be some changes he needs to make? Shouldn't he quit this, and start doing that? Jesus, you've got it all backwards. There needs to be some outward evidence of holiness or righteousness before he can publicly identify with you."* I don't know about you, but that sounds a lot like "church people" I've heard over the years.

It gets worse. Jesus heads to Matthew's house for dinner. I don't know how this happened and I wish we had more details. Matthew gets up to follow Jesus and I imagine the conversation went something like this.

Matthew:	*"Where are we going, Jesus?"*
Jesus:	*"To your house."*
Matthew:	*"Really? What are we going to do?"*
Jesus:	*"We're going to have a little dinner party."*
Matthew:	*"Okay. Who's coming?"*
Jesus:	*"Whoever you want to invite."*
Matthew:	*"Wow, I like following You, Jesus. I tried to follow the Pharisees but they had a thousand things I had to do and I couldn't even keep up with it. I choose to follow Jesus, we're having a party at my house and I get to invite my friends. This is new. This is different."*

To the religious leaders, the idea of Jesus going to Matthew's house was especially puzzling. Eating with tax collectors and sinners didn't make any sense. Shouldn't He tell them to repent, change their lives, and THEN follow Him? Why would He publicly associate with them before they've made any changes in their lives? Doesn't He have it backwards? **The invitation to follow Jesus is quite disturbing to religious people**. It's very disquieting to those who have grown content with a religious routine. Over time you can learn so much Bible, and you can get so religious that it's easy to begin categorizing those who aren't as religious as you.

Jesus responds to what they said and what they didn't say. *"Listen guys, I've come for the sake of people, not a game or a standard. You religious people are so caught up in doing everything right and making sure you're fine with God that you have overlooked the needs of people around you. I'm not caught up in getting people to live in a little box and get everything right all the time. That's not the point. I want a relationship, not some carbon copy of religion."* His response was the essence of why Jesus could ask someone like Matthew to follow Him. He knew his life was a mess. He invited him to come just the way he was and start riding and see where the journey went.

Jesus ends the conversation with these words, *"For I have not come to call the righteous, but sinners.'"* Isn't that great news? He invites me, you, and all who are on different levels of the righteous scale to follow Him. We are asked to start where we are, even if we are willing only to take Him home. You may be thinking there is something you need to do or not do. You may be wondering if there is a need to change this or fix that. Perhaps you assume there is a pattern to be copied and performed perfectly. Rest assured that is not how Jesus operates. Whatever you've done, and wherever you are, would you just follow Him? He may just want to go home with you and have a party with some of your friends. It may be simple. Would you just follow Jesus?

This invitation to follow Jesus is an invitation to a relationship. Because God loves you, He is committed to what is best for you. He wants to be in a relationship with you so He can influence you. He knows there do need to be some changes. There are some relationships you need to avoid, some habits you need to break, and some mistakes you need to repair. As a result, over time and at a very slow pace there will be change.

I am married to the most wonderful woman and mother in the world. After many years of marriage, I could write a list of things that I do habitually and even enjoy doing in my marriage now. If you had given me that list before I was married however, I might not have gotten married. There are a lot of things I do now for my wife and family that bring me great joy but if you had given me that list before marriage and before parenthood it would have scared me. I would have looked at that list and would have to have forced myself to do it. If it's going to take that to make her happy, if it's going to take that for my kids to grow up and be good kids, I don't know if I can do it. Do you know what happened? I fell in love. Through the years as my love and appreciation for my wife has deepened, I have changed. It has been more like "I love you" and "I want to please you" kind of change. It is no different with my kids. When there is a love relationship there are no patterns or rules, just acts of love.

God loves us so much, and as a result He knows there do need to be some changes. Even so, He invites you and me into a relationship that is characterized by following Him today. Don't worry about next year – just follow Him today. What you will discover is that in time there will be a transformation. In time there will be a brand new perspective on relationships, money, sex, dating. Eventually you will see work, time, and eternity in a totally different light. ALL of that will change, but don't worry about it now. Follow Jesus TODAY.

The invitation to follow Jesus is an invitation to the ride of your life. Imagine for a moment what happened because of Matthew's decision to follow Jesus. He had no idea what lay ahead for him. There were hundreds of other tax collectors just like him but we don't know their names. There were hundreds of people Jesus invited to follow Him and they refused, and we don't know who they were. Today, however, we name our kids after Matthew. We can read an unbelievable book in the Bible that bears his name. He had no idea what would happen because of his decision to follow Jesus. You and I have no idea what will happen every time God calls us out of our comfort zone to do something unique, or different, or to just follow Him.

If you're a high school student you have no idea what the result will be of your faithfulness to follow Jesus in your school. If you're a college student you have no idea how things may turn out because of your decision to follow Jesus rather than follow everybody else. If you're in business you have no idea what may come about with your decision to follow Jesus in your ethics and business decisions. Yes, there are some risks and there are some sacrifices. Those things are what the ride is about. It is the ride of your life because you have no idea what hangs in the balance of accepting the invitation to follow Jesus Christ.

In my line of work I hear all the bad stories. I've heard people tell me episode after episode of regret. I want to tell people if they had been following Jesus, He would have led them around that relationship. If they had been following Jesus, He would have led them away from that marriage. He would have led them away from debt, He would have led them away from that purchase, and He would have led them away from that job. If they would have been following Jesus they wouldn't be facing life with these regrets.

I have yet to meet anyone who has followed Jesus for years and years, and said it was a waste of time. I've never met or talked to anyone who had any regrets about following Jesus. Don't get me wrong. Following Jesus is going to cost you something, and we'll be talking about that in the next few chapters. Refusing to follow Jesus, however, will cost you a lot more. The reason we shy away from the ride of our life is that initial cost. You mean I have to leave my tax collector's booth and not even know where we're going? Yes, but if you say no to Jesus you have no idea what you have given up.

Are you at the place in life regardless of where you are – Christian or not even sure it's true – are you willing to accept the invitation to follow Jesus? He doesn't go too fast. He will be sensitive to where you are and what you know and don't know. He will be aware of your struggles and your life-style. If you accept the invitation to ride you will discover an unconditional acceptance by a loving, holy God. Before there is a list change orders, you will find yourself in a relationship that has the potential to transform you. Be prepared for the ride of your life.

CHAPTER 3

Taking It Slow

*"And as soon as they landed, they left every-
thing and followed Jesus."*

Luke 5:11 (TNIV)

For Matthew, following Jesus started by leaving his job and having Jesus at his house for a party. From there Matthew participates in the ride of his life. For others, following Jesus begins differently. Those who accept the invitation begin the ride of their lives and over time God does incredible things. They experience changes in their relationships, in their finances, in their families, and in their careers. However the ride begins, we eventually discover a very important truth. **Following Jesus is a process of moving from wherever we are to the next location He wants us to be.** Usually He takes the process slow, gradually moving us from where we are to the next place in our relationship with Him.

When I began to follow Jesus many years ago, I had no idea or any inclination that I would be a pastor. There was a desire to communicate but I used music and the arts as my medium. I was content to write and sing songs about my relationship with God. Over the next three decades God took me through the process of moving me from wherever I was to where I needed to be next. As I obeyed each change order and moved to the next destination, I found myself on the ride of my life. The next place for me after years of music ministry was to plant a church and become a pastor.

Many of you who are Christ followers have found yourselves in the process of God moving you to the next place as you follow Him. I think of my dear friend Tim Seippel who was a very successful salesman in the workplace. He accepted Jesus' invitation to follow Him and gradually God took him to the next place. He became a volunteer in ministry which led to being a part time College Pastor. At present he is a full time Community Pastor at our church. Tim is on the ride of his life. As each time Jesus asked him to move to the next place, Tim responded and followed Him. Those of you who have been Christ followers for some time can identify with that.

For some of you, however, that's sort of scary. Indeed, you may be thinking *"If I say yes to this ride and follow Jesus, He may want me to become a missionary to China or something."* That fear may be what is keeping you from following Jesus now. If He did want you to do something like that, I can assure you that over a slow process of moving from wherever you are to wherever you need to be, you will be ready to do it. I would like to show you what that process looks like because I don't want you to miss the ride of your life for any reason. You will see the invitation to follow Jesus is just awakening the next day and saying, *"God, where do you want me to follow You today? Just take me to the next location."*

This process can be seen in the New Testament when Jesus invites some common, everyday fishermen to follow Him. The Bible tells us they dropped everything right then and there and followed Jesus. These rugged fishermen left their nets, which means they left their occupations, and followed Jesus. James and John were in a family business with their father. Jesus said *"Follow Me"* and they left their father and the family business behind. That may sound more irresponsible than spiritual. It scares many of you because it seems too fast. Can't I do this a tiny bit at a time? Is it possible to take it a little slower? The answer is an absolute yes. Following Jesus is a process of moving from wherever we are to the next place in our relationship with Him. For many individuals, it's just simple baby steps. It's not realistic to initially meet Jesus then leave everything and become a missionary to China. What God wants from you as a follower is to simply take the next little step to the location where He wants you to be.

One day Jesus was teaching this huge crowd and they kept pressing Him to the water's edge. As He got closer and closer to the water, He noticed two boats and decided to utilize them. Water is a great conductor of sound, so why not use a natural amplification system? These fishermen had exactly what Jesus needed. Within this story we get a picture of the type of process God uses to move us to where we need to be next.

First, it is necessary to understand how they fished in those days. Fishing was done at night because the water was cooler and the fish would come to the surface. Nets were used for fishing and generally they would fish all night. Later they would come in, clean the fish, and get them ready for the day's market. Afterward they would clean their nets, mend them if they needed it, and spread them out to dry. Finally, they would roll them up, store them, and sleep the better part of the day because they had been up all night.

Apparently a seasoned fisherman named Peter was at the edge washing his nets or he might have been in the boat, we don't know. But it is highly likely that Peter had heard Jesus speak before and perhaps even witnessed some miracles. He probably knew that Jesus was a teacher and claimed to be sent from God. While Peter may have known about Jesus, Jesus certainly knew about Peter. At this point He wants to take Peter to the next place. He starts with something small. Jesus asks Peter to loan Him his boat. With Matthew it was just a party with friends. With Peter it was about using his boat and connecting in a small way.

Sometimes the next location is Jesus asking us to accomplish something small. Each time Jesus attempts to move us to the next location, it is always a matter of trust. It's an issue of believing He knows what is best for us. We must have faith that our relationship is at the place where we need to make a move. At times it's only a small, tiny step. Peter had been listening to Jesus, and now Jesus wanted Peter to do something small, like getting into the boat together. That may be where some of you are at this moment. You've been attending church or reading a book and you've been listening and learning about Jesus. Now He is asking you to trust him with something small, to go to the next destination in your relationship with Him. He may only be asking you to connect with Him a little closer. Perhaps it is only a matter of trusting His plan and purpose for your life and He simply wants you to step into the boat and go for a ride. It's not a matter of dying for Him, and it's not a matter of leaving everything immediately. Basically, He wants to start small and head to the next place. At times the next place may be a small step of getting a little closer to Him.

The next thing Jesus does is ask Peter to go fishing. I want you to imagine Peter's thoughts when Jesus says this. They had been fishing all night, which is when you're supposed to fish. They hadn't caught a thing. I don't know if Peter thought this, but I would have. *"Jesus, aren't You a carpenter? You need to understand that you don't fish in the daytime. The sun is up, the water is warm, and we just cleaned the nets. Besides that, there's a crowd watching. If these people see me fishing out there in the middle of the day they'll think I'm an idiot. This doesn't make any sense."* Peter may have thought it, but he didn't say it. I do love what he says next, because this is where a lot of us are. *"But if you say so, I'll let the nets down again."* I can only imagine what is going through Peter's head, *"Jesus, I wouldn't do this for anybody else. It doesn't make sense and I don't believe we're going to catch anything. But I've been listening to You and I've been watching You. I'm going to trust you. I may be the laughing stock of all of Galilee, but because you say so, I'll do it."* Peter takes a step of obedience and trust, and Jesus moves him to the next location in their relationship. He asks Peter to do something very specific.

Sometimes the next location is Jesus asking us do something specific. *"Peter, since we're in the boat, let's go fishing."* That required a little more faith and trust. Any good fisherman knows you don't fish during the daytime. You especially don't fish in the daytime when you didn't catch anything the night before. But Jesus plainly asks us to trust Him so we can move to the next place. Our response ought to be *"If you say so."* Peter obeyed and moved to a new destination in His relationship with Jesus. When he obeyed, something amazing happened. Peter's small faith intersected with Jesus' faithfulness and he realized who he was dealing with. He had seen Him before and he had heard Him teach. In that moment of obedience and trust, however, he realized who he was dealing with. At that instant not only did Peter realize who Jesus was; Peter realized that Jesus knew who Peter was. He probably knew things about Peter that nobody else knew. It was in that moment Peter discovered Jesus was no longer a teacher and no longer a prophet. He was the real, living, breathing Son of God. From that day on Peter would never be the same. It was just a matter of moving to the next place.

It is almost overlooked in the story, but the result of Peter's obedience of Jesus' specific request was a boat-load of fish. Their nets couldn't handle the enormous catch. Please understand the fish weren't the issue. The issue was trust. When God wants you to do something specific – to move out or move in, to stay or to go, to give or to keep – something happens when you trust Him. In time, when you see His faithfulness intersect with your faith, you discover there IS a God. He knows your name and He showed up in your life. The issue will not be the boyfriend, the girlfriend, the partnership, the money, or whatever is in your net. It's not about the fish. The issue is you trusted God and He acted on your behalf because He has a greater purpose for you. You moved from wherever you were to where you needed to be. That is the result of obedience when Jesus asks us to do something specific.

After the invitation to fish and experiencing the catch of the century, Jesus moves Peter to the next place. He invites Him to follow Him and become a fisher of men. Peter began by taking a small step and connecting with Jesus in a small way. He then took the next step of obeying a specific request to go fishing. There was only one thing left to do. When Jesus said, *"Follow Me"*, Peter left everything and followed Jesus. What else would you do? He left EVERYTHING and followed Him. Why? Peter realized Jesus had a bigger purpose for his life. **Sometimes the next location may be Jesus asking us to do something substantial.** Each step of obedience and trust leads us to connecting with God in a much larger way. As opposed to a category, God becomes personal. Like Peter, when Jesus reveals Himself to us, we discover that God can be known and God can be trusted. The fish in our nets do not matter anymore. Our small amount of faith crisscrossed with God's faithfulness and now we are poised to move toward a bigger and higher purpose.

Following Jesus is a process of moving from wherever you are to the next location He wants you to be. You may not be a religious person or a church person. The fact that you are reading this book is monumental for you. You're not ready to go fishing. You are just listening and learning, and there is certainly nothing wrong with that. You are exactly where God wants you to be and you may need to keep listening and learning for a while. There will come a day, however, when

God is going to nudge you and would like to borrow your boat. He will want you to get in for a ride. He will want you to step across the line of faith and trust Him with something small. It is time you let somebody know what's happening in your heart and you seek some spiritual wisdom. Talk with someone and ask them to pray with you. Speak to a pastor and get your questions answered. Taking small steps like these is moving to the next place.

There are many of you who have been following Jesus and He is asking you to do something specific. He may be asking you to move out of a relationship or stay in a marriage. He may be asking you to get out of a business partnership, become more generous, change the way you handle your time, or change your entertainment values. Whatever He is asks you to do, He is attempting to move you from where you are to where He wants you to be.

Do you know what I like about this story? This story is about all of us. We are somewhere in the process of God asking us to do something small, something specific, or something substantial. What is keeping us from moving to the next place in our relationship with Jesus Christ? The answer in one word is fear. Like Peter, we are terrified. Jesus knew Peter was afraid, and He knows when you're afraid. Jesus tells us there is nothing to fear. When you and I decide to follow Jesus, He takes responsibility for the outcome of the ride. We have no reason to be afraid. I still remember the fear I felt when God wanted me to leave where I was and do something else. After being a worship leader for years in a comfortably large church that took good care of my family, God said it was time to go to the next place. It was a scary thing. I could have said *"No, that's too much and too far. That's too risky and I can't see the future. How am I going to make a living?"* Very easily I could have refused His invitation to take me to the next place.

Every time I look back at how close I was to doing the

safe, sensible thing and staying where I was, I get down on my knees before God. I thank Him for pushing me beyond my comfort zone and moving me to the next place. What if I had missed out on all the people that I've met, the lives that have been changed, and the things I've seen God do? I had no idea what the result of that decision would be back then. Peter had no idea where the ride would take him due to his decision to trust Jesus. You have no idea what the outcome of your decision to follow Christ will be. The greatest tragedy in life is missing this experience of letting God move you to the next location in your relationship with Him. Don't carry the regret of living your life and never knowing what God might do if you were to step out and trust Him. You don't want to miss what could be the ride of your life!

CHAPTER 4

My Way Or The Highway

*"Then Peter said to him, 'We've given up
everything to follow you. What will we get?'"*

Matthew 19:27 (TNIV)

If we were honest, many of us came to Jesus because
something was broken and needed fixing - marriages,
kids, finances, careers - it could be any number of things.
There are times in our lives when we come to God for what
we can get from God. He is amazingly patient with us but
eventually along the way on this ride you and I are going to
learn an important truth. **There is a big difference between
using Jesus and following Jesus.** There is a huge distinc-
tion between trying to use Jesus to obtain what you want and
following Him.

Somewhere along the ride there will be a moment of truth
for you as there has been for me. The time will come when
your agenda will clash with His, and you will be required to
make a choice. You must decide if you are in this for you, or if
you are willing to lay down your personal agenda and simply
follow Him because He is God. Competing agendas lead to
conflict. Those of us who are or have been married have had
those times when we were excited about the direction of how
something was going, and discovered our spouse was excited
about something in a different direction. Competing agendas

31

in families always lead to conflict. Somebody has to give up their agenda and go along with what everybody else is going to do. The only way to avoid conflict or the break up of any relationship is for somebody to lay down their agenda.

The same is true in our relationship with God. Somewhere en route, as God moves us at that slow pace, there are going to be competing agendas. The good news is there are people in the Bible who were much like us. Jesus' disciples had their own agendas at times. James and John, for instance, asked Jesus if they could sit on his right and left when he started His kingdom. If that's not trying to leverage your relationship with Jesus, I don't know what is. Peter came to Jesus not too long afterward and asked Jesus a question. *"Jesus, we've forsaken everything to follow you. What will we get?"* In other words, he wanted to know what was in it for Peter. He was reminding Jesus he had left his fishing business to follow. Peter is no different than us. He was along for the ride and following Jesus, but he was also trying to obtain something for himself.

When Jesus was arrested before His crucifixion, the disciples ran for the hills. Being arrested wasn't in their plans. Things weren't going their way and they hightailed and ran. After the resurrection Jesus gathered them together and gave them a second chance. They learned that along the way on the ride of your life you have to lay down your agenda. The disciples made the change and laid down their agendas, and eventually their lives to follow Jesus. There was one exception - Judas. Judas was not willing to make the turn. He started off as selfish and immature in following Jesus as the other guys did. Unlike the rest, however, something happened in Judas. He wasn't able to go the distance.

Like many others, Judas saw Jesus as the Messiah, as somebody who had been sent by God. There was an Old Testament framework that indicated God was sending a Messiah who would deliver Israel. He would lead Israel to once again be a superpower. Thereafter all nations would acknowledge Israel's God. When Jesus appeared on the scene the disciples knew He was the Messiah. No one else could do what He did and talk the way He talked. If they could stay close to Jesus, eventually He's going to proclaim Himself king and Israel would be a great nation again. Those closest to Jesus could be right up there at the top with the king. With that in mind they hang out with Jesus, biding their time and waiting for the kingdom to come. They would ask Him from time to time, *"Is now the time for the kingdom to come? You're always talking about the kingdom, but when is the kingdom coming?"* Judas saw Jesus in this way, and he thought the best way to leverage his life and his time was being around the one who would soon be the king.

On the other hand, there were some problems with Jesus. Jesus didn't really seem to hate the Romans enough for Judas. He rarely said anything negative about the nation that certainly the Messiah would overthrow. In addition to that issue, Jesus wouldn't get organized. They weren't raising money to start an army. He also kept making all the religious leaders mad, which wasn't working too well. You need to have allies to overthrow Rome and establish a kingdom. Jesus kept alienating himself from certain people among the Jews. Consequently, there were things about Jesus that didn't fit into Judas' pattern. Still, he kept waiting.

Ultimately, there came a time when Judas couldn't handle it anymore. He was not getting what he wanted out of following Jesus. He decided to take matters into his own hands. Judas and Jesus had competing agendas. Rather than misunderstanding Jesus' plan but subscribing to it anyway, He makes a choice. Basically, Judas said, *"If you're not going to do it my way, then it's the highway for me. I'm taking over because I'm not getting what I thought I would get out of this deal."* His agenda becomes clear when a woman brings an alabaster jar of expensive perfume and pours it on

Jesus. Mark's account says this perfume was worth about a year's wages. In this day and age it would be like paying $50,000 or more for an expensive and rare perfume to dump on someone's head. John also tells this story and gives additional details. He says Judas was directly in the middle of this conversation and started a discussion.

Judas thought it was a waste and when he saw this, he stirred up the rest of the disciples. He was adamant that this perfume could have been used to give money to the poor. How were they ever going to get anywhere if every time they had something valuable they kept using it, giving it away, or wasting it? This was no way to start a kingdom. Although Judas was behind all this, he wasn't planning to give the money to the poor. He was saving it and actually stealing it. Obviously, Jesus knows this and alludes to the fact that the perfume is simply preparation for Jesus' burial. That was the last straw for Judas. If Jesus not going to save some money to build a war chest, he was done. If He was allowing this sort of thing to happen over and over, he had had enough. Jesus was never going to be Messiah if He kept acting like this. They would never have a kingdom if Jesus kept operating this way. It made no sense at all. Judas was wasting his time following Jesus. From that time on Judas sought an opportunity to betray Jesus. He had gone as far as he was willing to go. What he was after and what Jesus was after were not the same. He tried to pressure, force, and manipulate Jesus to be what he wanted, but then he took matters into his own hands.

You know how the story ends, but in just a few short days Judas learned two very important lessons. They are lessons that some of us will learn the easy way and some of us will learn the hard way. **First, you cannot force God to do something He doesn't desire to do.** Judas was determined to have his way even if it meant betraying the Son of God. He was going to force Jesus to let the world know who He truly was. Perhaps he thought at some point during the arrest or the trial Jesus would throw off his robe and be in His king costume. Surely He wouldn't allow Himself to be tried. Certainly He wouldn't allow Himself to be condemned. They would never put Him to death for these trivial things He's done. Judas learned you can't force God to do something He doesn't want to do.

Second, you cannot stop God from doing what He wants to do. You can't manipulate Him or do something in such a way as to bypass or sidetrack His will. Eventually within this process Judas learned what a fool he had been. When it didn't go down like he thought it would, he attempted to right the wrong. He tried to give the money back to the priests and elders. Their reaction was cold and calculated, *"That's your problem, Judas. You made the decision, you live with it."* Judas had failed miserably to correct his mistake. There was no one else to turn to and nothing more he could do.

If you decide to follow Jesus, at some point in your life there will be an event, a relationship, or a decision where your agenda and God's agenda will not line up. You will either break yourself trying to force His hand to carry out something He will not do, or break yourself trying to keep Him from doing something He has intended to do. If you are a Christ follower and you are in a battle with God over something like a personal relationship, an issue at work, or whatever your agenda is, be warned. This is what you must understand if you insist on your agenda. **YOU are responsible for the consequences of refusing to follow Jesus.** You are liable for the outcome of your decision. Like Judas, you own it all, and you are on your own. When you say no to Jesus' invitation to follow, you are thinking you can control the outcome of a ride you've never been on. There are some decisions you make that you cannot unmake. You must realize forgiveness is not the issue. Consequence is the issue.

When you say no to God's agenda and insist on your agenda you take responsibility for the outcome of the ride. Do you really want to do that?

Judas knew he couldn't go running back to Jesus. He couldn't go back to the religious leaders. Judas had no place to go; he was on his own. All of us know what happened. Judas took his own life. **If we learn anything from the tragedy of Judas we need to learn refusing to follow Jesus leads to self destructive behavior.** Saying no to Jesus will move you in the direction of destructive relationships and destructive lifestyles. When you move beyond the source of life, and the source of love, and the source of forgiveness, you are not moving toward ANYTHING good. You are heading toward destructive behavior, destructive relationships, and destructive habits. When you do, you will be exactly where Judas was, filled with remorse and with no place to go. Say no to Jesus and you say no to everything that makes life worth living and the ride worth taking.

There is a big difference between using Jesus and following Jesus. If you are facing a competing agenda with God, you should do the same thing Jesus did when He had a conflicting agenda. One night in a garden He prayed so hard that the Bible says He sweated drops of blood. The issue was you and me. Jesus didn't want to die for sin. Nevertheless He prayed *"Not My will, but Your will be done."* He laid down His agenda for that of His Heavenly Father. My prayer is that you will do the same and lay down your agenda, knowing that God will take responsibility for the outcome of the ride.

CHAPTER 5

Cross Roads

*"If any of you wants to be my follower, you
must turn from your selfish ways, take up
your cross, and follow me."*

Mark 8:34 (TNIV)

There is a scene in my life that I live over and over. It was literally a moment in time, as it lasted barely sixty seconds. On a crisp, autumn Friday night in a small Texas town, the hometown crowd had gathered once again for the King of Sports in the Lone Star State - football. *"Friday Night Lights"* was no imaginary television show. It was for real and I was a part of it. Playing football was something I loved and was fortunate enough to be good at it. At the end of my junior year I had scholarship letters from almost all the colleges in the Southwest Conference as well as others. All I needed to do was survive my senior year unscathed and I had a football scholarship awaiting me and hopefully, a stint in the pros in the future. Now midway through my senior season, I was counting the games and the days until graduation.

In the stands that night was a special guest. A beautiful brunette cheerleader I had met at a different school had come to see me play while her team was off that week. It was definitely one of those Football Captain/Cheerleader relationships you see a lot in high school. All I knew was when my blue eyes met her green eyes for the first time, I saw AQUA! This would be the only chance she could see me play in high school. I wanted to live up to her expectations. That night I discovered love can make you do crazy things.

Our team scored first, but not until early in the second quarter. While I played defense, I was also the kicker. After kicking the extra point, we prepared to line up to kick off. Now comes the moment. For some reason I looked up in the stands, saw that cheerleader and made a decision. A kicker's job is to kick the ball and then wait around in case the ball carrier slips by everyone else. I decided I was going to run down the middle of the field and make the tackle. It was a plan I was sure would impress that pretty girl watching. My mind made up, I kicked the ball and ran as fast as I could down the middle of the field. I threw off one blocker, who I think was surprised to see me, and headed straight to where I saw the ball descending into waiting hands. My timing was impeccable. A second after the ball was caught, I made a textbook hit in the numbers and began to drive the ball carrier backwards. He tried to spin but I held fast, only by now the rest of the team had joined me for the kill.

The power of four or five other tacklers found me still holding on but moving backwards. Before I knew it I was about to be on the bottom of the pile instead of the top. As I went down, a sound in my ankle pierced the air. I was sure everyone in the stadium heard it that night. After the other players stood, I was still on the ground writhing in pain. A few minutes later they helped me off the field, hopping on one leg. Thankfully, the ankle had not broken, but several ligaments had been torn. It was an injury that would take a long time to recover from. Rehabilitation would not happen fast enough. Sports medicine in that day was archaic compared to sports medicine today.

What was I thinking? I had made a terrible decision.

As a matter of fact, it turned out to be a life changing decision. There were no more college offers. I made the decision to give up football to pursue something else. Gone were the dreams of playing in the NFL. In less than a minute, my whole world turned upside down and my future went a totally different direction. Years later I still replay that scene in my mind. I catch myself asking the "what if" and "why me" questions. In what measured up to be a moment in time, I neglected to do something very important: I did not keep the end in mind. When we neglect to keep the end in mind, many times we make decisions we later regret. It applies to numerous areas. How different would our decisions be about dating, marriage, career, and morality if we just kept the end in mind? Among the hardest things to teach our children is the concept of keeping the end in mind. In our world of instant gratification, it is difficult for them to see beyond the moment, beyond the now. Time after time we choose to operate in the present with no thought for the future.

You may be wondering what happened to the cheerleader. Despite my failed attempt at showing off, she married me a few years later. We have five wonderful children, and I traded a life of football for a life of love and ministry. Each of us enjoy our own journey of following Jesus, and for that I am truly thankful. I may have lost something I truly wanted, but I gained something better. At times life throws at us the dilemma of choosing to lose one thing that we may gain something better. It's a predicament we can all identify with. The tragedy is that many choose to ignore keeping the end in mind. In the future, when they are older, they would give anything to go back and make a different and better decision.

You and I face the same challenge today as Christ followers when Jesus asks us to follow Him. Even when you're just beginning and it means nothing more than attending church, you are still relinquishing your Sundays. That may be where you are. You are just starting this ride. For others who may be way down the road following Christ it may mean a different challenge. The decision may be about discontinuing a relationship, staying in a marriage, making financial resources available, or volunteering in ministry. It's almost like we have to die because we must lose a part of our lives. At the same time, however, we know that when we're old we would forgo everything between now and then to be able to return to that day and do the right thing. We would give up everything to live our lives in such a way that they reflected issues of eternity and not our selfish little world.

As Jesus neared the end of His ministry it became very evident to the disciples that "happily ever after" wasn't close to happening. He started mentioning His death. Although He also referred to a resurrection, they never seemed to hear that part. They couldn't get past the death talk. Suddenly it wasn't fun to follow Jesus anymore. They began to have reservations and there is this scene in the life of His disciples and followers where Jesus confronts them with a dilemma where they must make a choice. In a very direct and straightforward way Jesus tells them, *"Following Me will cost you something. But refusing to follow Me could cost you everything. Matthew, you gave up your job of collecting taxes. Peter, James, John, you quit your fishing business. You already know that following Me costs you something. But I'm warning you. Refusing to follow Me could cost you everything."* If I may paraphrase, this is the essence of what Jesus was saying: **Following Jesus may cost you your life, but your life will not lose its meaning.** In other words, if you don't follow Jesus now, there will be a time in life when you would concede everything to revert back and make the decision to follow Him. Even though you may have lived a life with more fame and fortune than you ever dreamed, at some point in your advancing years you would forgo everything you experienced to be able to come back and relive your life and follow Jesus. It is in following Him that we find true meaning.

This talk of Jesus' death didn't set well with the disciples, especially Peter. One day Jesus asked his disciples who people were saying He was. They told him that some said He was John the Baptist, and some said He was Elijah or one of the other prophets. Then Jesus asked them who they thought He was. Peter made this bold statement and said *"You are the Messiah."* Remember, Peter had the same mindset about the Messiah all the other Jews had. They thought the Messiah was coming to overthrow Rome and make Israel the kingdom it once was. Yet Jesus mentioned suffering and rejection and dying. That's not Messiah talk. After this bold admission in front of the other guys that He was the Messiah, Peter sort of scolded Jesus. *"You can't talk like this and expect to be successful in becoming King."* Peter's reprimand struck a nerve with Jesus, and He chastised Peter. *"You don't think I know why you and everyone else are following Me? You don't think I know that you and everyone else are gunning for some position in a fantasy kingdom that you know nothing about? You don't think I know, Peter that you are in this for you?"*

What Jesus says to Peter He says to you and me. **The ride of your life is not about you.** If you want to strike a nerve with Jesus, try following Him for what you can get out of it. It is so opposite of the love and nature of God. When God sent His Son it was not about Him, it was about you. When Jesus died on the cross, it was not about Him, it was about you. When He carried the weight of your sin and my sin on that cross it was about everybody BUT Him. You may not know it yet or understand it yet, but the ride of your life is not about you. Therefore, Jesus draws a line in the sand and offers the challenge, *"If any of you wants to be My follower, you must turn from your selfish ways, take up your cross, and follow Me."* If you commit to follow Jesus there will be times when you will need to turn from your selfish ways and lay down your agenda. You will be called upon to deny yourself and say yes to God. In our culture this isn't a popular thing. Every time you switch on the television, open a magazine, or look at a billboard it tells you not to deny yourself. Culture says you should indulge yourself. Every media medium tells you to have everything and have it now because you deserve it. Instead of encouraging you to deny yourself, you are being pushed to do the opposite.

Jesus goes even further and says not only do you deny yourself but you must die to yourself. He uses the phrase "take up your cross". In that culture the cross had death all over it. In that society a cross wasn't artwork or something they hung around their neck. A cross had a smell to it, a feel to it, and a sight to it. They had seen a cross used, and Jesus knew that. Consequently He utilized one of the most graphic of all word pictures to communicate that at some point if you choose to follow Him, you will have to die to yourself. You will have to take up your cross to follow Him.

That's extremely threatening, isn't it? Especially when you don't know where you are going and what He is asking you to do. It's not very smart to sign up for a ride and not even know where you are going. Why would He make such a demand? It's because if there comes a time when He asks you to do something and you don't want to do it, there is a sense where it's all about you. You tell God to disappear because it is your relationship. You tell God not to interfere because it is your money. You tell God to get lost because it is your college major. Those are your friends, your decisions, and your plans. Jesus warns us: If you live your life saying no to Me in order to save your life, you will eventually lose that life. You are spending a lot of your time and energy trying to preserve something you will lose anyway. In time, what you keep for your own selfish reasons will be lost anyway.

As threatening as it sounds, Jesus is inviting us to something. He issues us a higher calling, a deeper purpose, a nobler cause - His cause. **The ride of your life is about the cause of Christ.** You will someday lose your life anyway because we all die. But if you choose to lose your life for Christ's sake, you will actually preserve it. Follow Jesus and you may lose your life, but your life doesn't need to lose its meaning. What you gain from years of following Jesus nobody can take away. How much wiser it is to make the short term decision with long term implications. The ride of your life is about the cause of Christ and the cause of Christ has eternal implications.

It is so important that we keep the end in mind in our decisions to follow or not to follow. As I consider what Jesus is asking I know it appears like He is demanding a lot. Sure it seems we must deny ourselves and even die to ourselves. But what a tragedy it would be to spend your whole life defining yourself by decisions where you said no to God. You will spend your whole life becoming what you may have wanted and in an instant you will lose it. In addition you will forego the significance that following Jesus brings.

Following Jesus may cost you your life, but your life will not lose its meaning. You will lose your life anyway. Follow Jesus now and in that moment in time when this life stops, you will be who you were meant to be. Yes, you will need to give up some things. Yes, it will seem like you are dying. But you will never someday look back with regrets and wish you had this moment to decide to get in on the ride. If you're not up to the ride, that's fine. Jesus is not trying to scare you. You can say no to Jesus and revert to the life and reputation that you build for yourself. Jesus is simply offering you an invitation. It's an invitation to a life that will never lose its meaning if you will follow Him. It's an invitation to the ride of your life.

CHAPTER 6

Detour Signs

*"I am the light of the world. Whoever fol-
lows me will never walk in darkness, but will
have the light of life."*

John 8:12 (TNIV)

Some years ago I had the privilege of traveling to Scotland to play golf. The sport of golf was born in Scotland at a course called St Andrews. The British Open is played there and at eight other courses in Scotland and England. I was able to visit the course but didn't have a chance to play it. However, I was scheduled to play at Carnoustie, one of the other British Open courses in Scotland. A good friend of mine and I made this trip in three days. We flew into Aberdeen from Houston, Texas and drove to Carnoustie on the northeast coast. When we arrived we discovered that we had time to play a round, although we were only scheduled to play the next day. Since we had just arrived there was no time to unpack before our tee time. My golf shoes were in my golf bag but my thick athletic socks were in my suit-case at the hotel. Thinking it was no big deal, I put my golf shoes on with my thin dress socks. What I didn't consider was at Carnoustie there are no golf carts. You walk the entire course with a caddy. But I was in Scotland, I was playing at Carnoustie, and I was walking on the same hallowed ground as Jack Nicklaus, Arnold Palmer, Tiger Woods, and so many others. Who cared if I still had my slacks on and my socks were thin and black?

It was at the 10th hole I felt the blister coming on the back of my heel. By hole 13 I was walking with a limp, and it really affected my game. I couldn't plant my foot well so I wasn't able to swing correctly, which took the ball to far away places. Hitting it out of the fairway, I was now walking even more. Stopping was not an option at this point. This was Carnoustie and I was playing one of my dream courses. I tried to compensate by walking mostly on the balls of my feet. This put an extraordinary strain on my toes, and by hole 17 I had a blister on the side of my big toe. With extreme pain I played the 18th hole and finished. Had it been any other day on any other course I would have quit and headed home. However, a chance like this doesn't occur very often. When I returned to the hotel to see the damage, it was hard to believe how small that blister on my heel was. I could have sworn it was huge. The one on my toe was even smaller. Yet both of them caused extreme pain, and at any other course here in the states I would have called it quits. It didn't matter that my other foot was okay or my arms were okay and I could swing a club. It didn't matter that my back was healthy and I could bend over and tee the ball up or get it out of the hole. Despite the fact that the rest of my body worked fine, there was no way to compensate for a little less than a square inch piece of flesh on the back of my heel. Those blisters were obstacles that shot down my game.

In your decision to follow Jesus and participate in the ride of your life, along the way there will be obstacles. From your vantage point they may seem very small, like that blister. When you meet those obstacles you will do what I did that day at Carnoustie. You will try to compensate. Obstacles will turn up along the way and there will be no way to compensate for them. **If you want to follow Jesus,**

you must remove the obstacles rather than compensate for them. Throughout this ride we're describing you will run into some things - a relationship, a habit, a hobby, a schedule - whatever it is it will be a hindrance to following Christ. The Bible is very clear about a correlation between removing obstacles and our ability to follow Christ. If certain obstacles are not removed, you will find yourself running off the road or taking a detour. Ultimately you will wind up in a destination you didn't wish to be.

You will recall those times with regret and wonder what happened. As you trace them back you will find situations that became obstacles. Everything was great until you met that guy or girl. Things were fine until you took that job. Life was good until you made that purchase. You will find you didn't remove those obstacles, you compensated for them. You met up with an obstacle - a relationship, a job, a circumstance - and it made you detour from following Christ. Now you are left with scars and memories that you wish you could return and undo. It happens because you tried to compensate rather than remove the obstacle. You need to get back on the road and into the ride.

The writer of the book of Hebrews describes following Christ much like a race. The words are clear. *"Therefore, since we are surrounded by such a great cloud of witnesses, let us throw off everything that hinders and the sin that so easily entangles. And let us run with perseverance the race marked out for us."* (Hebrews 12:1 TNIV) As you follow Christ you will learn to discern the will of God for your life. Gradually you will gain knowledge of what's right and what's wrong, what God wants you to do and what He doesn't want you to do. There is a course, a ride God has marked out for you and the boundaries are clear. The goal is to remain on the road that is marked out for you. Staying on the road enables you to reach the end of your life and look back at a life well lived. Remaining on course allows you to experience a marriage well managed, kids well raised, and money well handled. If you want to ride the road that is marked out for you, you must do away with everything that hinders and the sin that so easily entangles.

We are given two categories. First, there is everything that hinders. A definition for "hinders" would be "an impediment to progress". Basically, it's anything that obstructs our path. An obstacle is not necessarily something bad. **Some obstacles are good things, just not good for us.** Because of your personality, age, or stage of life, some things may be good, just not good for you. Due to your past some things are not good for you. They may not be hindrances to other people, but they are hindrances to you. You may be in a relationship or a friendship that on the outside looks good. Eventually it may well become a barrier in your obedience to God. Because of your past, present, and future it may interfere with you becoming everything God wants you to be. Even if there's not a Bible verse about it, you know in your heart that relationship is a barrier to following Christ. You need to remove the hindrance, not make adjustments for it.

I can suggest some possible obstacles. Nobody knows but you whether they are obstacles that hinder you or not. Although they are not "sins", or there isn't a Bible verse about them, you will try to compensate instead of eradicate. Along with some relationships, certain forms of entertainment might be an obstacle for you. There are certain environments that could be obstacles. It may be certain hobbies or possessions that get in the way. There is nothing bad about those things, but for some people they interfere with the ride God has for them.

The second category is things that entangle us. Those are the more obvious things there are Bible verses about and things you hear pastors and teachers warn us about. **Some obstacles are bad things, and are very bad for us.** Even when it relates to sin, the temptation is to compensate rather than remove. The warning is clear: You can't compensate for sin. It will run you off the road. God has marked out for you the ride of your life and you don't want something so small and inconsequential to take you on a detour or have you crash and burn. This is why it is so important to remove obstacles as opposed to compensating for them.

All obstacles, good or bad, take our focus off of following Jesus. When we stop focusing on following Jesus and try to compensate for the obstacles, it diverts, delays, and eventually destroys the ride God has mapped out for us. Don't make the mistake of trading the relationship with the God with whom you will spend eternity for a short term relationship that leaves you with only bad memories and scars. As painful as it is, the wisest thing you can do is remove the relationship with that person in order to maintain the relationship with your Savior.

Once again, in following Jesus we must remove the obstacles instead of compensating for them. Many of you at this moment are in so much debt because you compensated rather than removed bad spending habits. Some of you are so unhappy in your marriage because you compensated instead of terminating the relationship before you married. Many of you are stuck with a job you hate because you compensated instead of eliminating the bad choice. The only way to insure you are still on track and still following Christ in the years ahead is to remove these obstacles, not compensate for them. If you try to compensate, it will detour your ride.

CHAPTER 7

The Man Who Refused The Ride

*"'Go and sell all your possessions and give
the money to the poor, and you will have
treasure in heaven. Then come, follow me.'
At this the man's face fell, and he went
away very sad, for he had many
possessions."*

Mark 10:21b-22 (TNIV)

In the 1960's I grew up watching the popular show "Let's Make A Deal". Each episode of the show consisted of several "deals" between the host and a member or members of the audience as traders. Audience members were chosen at the host's whim as the show moved along, and couples were often selected to play together as traders. The deals were mini-games within the show that took several formats. In the simplest format, a contestant was given a prize of medium value and the host offered them the opportunity to trade for another prize. However, the offered prize was unknown. It may have been concealed on the stage behind one of three curtains, behind "boxes" onstage, or occasionally in other forms. The initial prize given to the trader may also have been concealed, such as in a box, wallet or purse, or the contestant may have initially been given a box or curtain. The format varied widely.

As I look back at that show, it brings to mind some observations as they relate to following Christ and the ride of your life. For example, the LESS you have, the EASIER it is to trade for the unknown. If all you have is a paper clip, it's easier to exchange thinking the unknown ought to be better. It's an easy decision. But if you have a television or a vacation trip, is it worth trading for what's behind Door Number One? When you're 14 and you hear the invitation from Jesus to follow and trust Him with everything, what do you really have to give? When you're young, you don't have a lot that you can "trade" to God. When you're 50, however, it's quite a bit different. I have cars, a motorcycle, a house, some furniture, and kids in college. I have a lot of stuff. Thus, the MORE you have, the HARDER it is to trade for the unknown.

When it comes to following Jesus, pursuing possessions can keep you from having the ride of your life. One of the greatest hindrances to following Jesus is the pursuit and management of our possessions - from cars to bank accounts, from homes to investment portfolios. Don't get me wrong. Your wealth and your possessions do not bother God. He is only troubled by anything that stands in the way of Him being the Lord and the boss of your life. God is not against you having stuff. It doesn't matter if it's a car or a car factory. He is more concerned that the stuff interferes with following Him. All of us run the risk of letting our pursuit of possessions keep us from the ride of our lives.

In the New Testament Jesus encounters a man who refused the ride of his life. Jesus invited him to follow and he refused. He is the only one in Scripture we know of that basically turned down the invitation. The story is commonly referred to as the story of the rich young ruler. This man runs up to Jesus one day and falls to his knees asking, *"Good Teacher, what must I do to inherit eternal life?* He had done all he knew to do. Yet there was something on the inside of him that said he had to do something else to make God approve of him. To him there was something more to getting that eternal life everyone was interested in. He is asking Jesus, *"How do I get inside and how do I know I can get inside? Tell me what I need to do."* Jesus uses this opportunity to discover what this fellow actually thought about Him. He called Jesus a good teacher. What did he mean by good? Did he see Jesus as God-like or as God Himself? Was he buying into what he heard Jesus teach? Perhaps Jesus paused to let him answer. If he believed that Jesus was God that takes you in one direction. If he believes he is only a good person that takes you in another direction.

Apparently he saw Jesus as merely a good teacher. It was possible He originated from God, but certainly wasn't God or God's son. There wasn't anything that special about Him. Once Jesus recognizes it He did the only thing He could do. Rather than explaining to Him how to have eternal life through faith, He sends him back to the law. There is a reason He did that. This young man did not sense he needed a Savior. He sensed he needed something else to do. *"Just give me the right TO DO list, Jesus, and I will get it DONE. Then I can have eternal life and God will say I DID fine. Show me the pattern, the sequence, or whatever. What do I need to DO?"* He didn't approach Jesus saying, *"I'm a dirty, wretched sinner and I need someone to save me and forgive me."* This young man was not after forgiveness. He was searching for peace. Somehow with all he had done it was still insufficient.

Jesus points him to the law. Keeping the law will give you plenty to do. But this young man knew the law. Every Jewish male knew it from childhood. He tells Jesus, *"I want you to know I've kept the whole law since I was a boy."* The implication was there was still something wrong. He still didn't have peace. He had done all he knew to do. What else could he DO to have eternal life? Jesus observes this guy and instantly feels compassion for him. This man is genuine and very serious. He really desires to have eternal life but he has one problem: He thinks he's perfect. He really believes he's kept the law perfectly. Jesus' heart goes out to him and He gives him the opportunity of a life time. If the story had gone differently, we might have known this man's name.

What Jesus offers this fellow boggles the mind. In essence, He offers him what he offered Peter that day when He asked him to leave his nets and follow Him. It's the same thing he offered Matthew that day at the tax table. He invites him to the ride of his life. Jesus says, *"I think your heart is right. I think you really wish to know the truth so I'll give you the truth. Let Me help you finally answer your question. You will need to do the one thing you haven't done. Go sell all your possessions, give the money to the poor, and come follow Me."* He just needed to DO one thing. Here's what I think Jesus meant by the one thing. On another occasion Jesus was asked what the greatest commandment was. He didn't say it was honor your father and mother, don't commit adultery, or don't steal. He didn't quote any of the top ten. Instead, Jesus said the greatest commandment is to love God with all your heart, and love people as much as you love yourself. The greatest commandment has to does with love, not a "to do" list. It's about a relationship, not a game of "Copy God". The best thing one could do from Jesus' perspective was to love God and love people.

Sadly, this guy was not about love at all. He was about a "to do" list. For him it was not about love, or a relationship, or a pursuit of intimacy. It wasn't about doing anything for anybody else. For the rich young ruler, it was all about him. As a result Jesus tells him his heart is right but there is something missing. He gave him the opportunity to obtain what was missing. *"Go sell all your possessions and give the money to the poor."* That would take care of loving people. *"Then, come follow Me."* That accomplishes loving

God with all your heart. All he had to DO was get rid of all that stuff and follow Jesus. If he had done that, at the end of the journey he would have discovered what it meant to have eternal life. Jesus' words resonate to all who are seeking a "to do" list for eternal life. Do you want something to do? Dispose of all that stuff you're so wrapped up in. Separate yourself from all the things that support your sense of arrogance and self sufficiency. Divest yourself of everything that supports that notion in you that you don't need anything else and you have it all together. Then come and follow Jesus and at the end of this ride you will understand what is missing.

There was no happy ending for this young man. He refused the ride because the Bible says he had too many possessions. His possessions kept him from having the ride of his life. It is a tragedy but how many of us do the same thing? If we had encountered Jesus back in the "I don't have much" day, we would have traded our little to follow Him. Now we have way too much stuff. We can't follow Him. If we were honest, this story scares a lot of us. We have a lot of possessions. Does that mean we have to give them up? Allow me to remove your fear right now. You are not required to sell everything you have to follow Jesus. Do I hear a sigh of relief? The fact is, you and I have been required to do far less, and we still don't do it. We've been asked to do far less than liquidate everything and march off on some ride with a guy on a road where we don't know where He's going. All we've been asked to do in the Bible is to think in terms of stewardship. Everything belongs to God anyway, and as stewards we are to give a percentage of what has been given to us on a consistent basis. Most of us won't even part with that. If you are a Christ follower, the pursuit of "stuff" can hinder you from the ride of your life.

Possessions cause us to focus on ourselves. When we focus only on ourselves it affects our relationships. Possessions influence how you relate to your spouse and to your kids. They will have an effect on any relationship you have. Following Jesus means you are required to love the people around you. Following Jesus means you must treat your spouse a certain way. You cannot be a great husband or wife and be totally absorbed with possessions. Your relationships with other people and your relationship with God suffer.

Possessions keep us from serving others. Most of us thought when we were younger if we ever had a lot of money, we would have more time to help other people. But now that we have more money we have less time to serve other people. Why is that? It's because the pursuit of possessions has the potential to pull us away from service to others and concentrate on serving ourselves.

Possessions keep us from giving generously. How many of us said when we were younger if I had a lot of money I could help this organization or I could help this person or this group? Research tells us the more a person's income increases, the less percentage they give away. Pursuit of possessions has the potential to keep us from giving generously, despite the fact that we have more to give. The further you descend on the income level, the more money people give. If you have less, you are more willing to trade it for the unknown. Having more makes it harder to trade for the unkown.

Possessions prevent us from having an eternal perspective. When you acquire a lot of stuff on this earth, you don't think much about heaven. On the other hand, there are people on this earth that have so little, they can't wait for heaven. Some of us are so focused on possessions that if life ended and heaven was our destiny, it would be an interruption. It is hard to have an eternal perspective when you have so much.

My final thought as we conclude this chapter is a warning. Our pursuit of possessions can keep us from the ride of our life. God loves us so much He offers you and me the opportunity of a lifetime to follow Him and find a life worth living. He doesn't want anything to stand in the way or hinder that ride. He knows you have needs and He recognizes you have kids to feed. He understands you have bills to pay. He also knows the less you have the easier it is to trade it for the unknown. The issue with Jesus is not your possessions or your money. The issue is anything that stands between you and following Jesus and Him being Lord of your life. If we are truthful, most of the time the biggest obstacle is our pursuit of things. Don't be the person who lets possessions stand in the way of the ride of your life.

CHAPTER 8

Changing Direction

*"Instantly the man could see, and he
followed Jesus down the road."*

Mark 10:52b (TNIV)

C hristian History was a required class for me in college. I was grateful to have a good professor who had the ability to make things interesting. I took other classes from him because I liked him a lot and he became one of my mentors. We were discussing one day the need for change in the church to really impact the world. At my age I was into creative methods and innovation which kept things fresh. Like many of my student peers, I thought I could change the world. However, I could not understand why people were reluctant to change, and at times even adamant of their dislike for what I was doing. My professor gave me a quote that is on the tomb of a Bishop in Westminster Abbey from 1100 AD. This is what the inscription says, *"When I was young and free and my imagination had no limits I dreamed of changing the world. As I grew older and wiser and realized the world would not change I shortened my sights somewhat and decided to change only my country: but it too seemed immovable. As I grew into my twilight years I settled on changing only my family and those closest to me, but alas they would have none of it. Now as I lay on my deathbed I suddenly realize that if I had only changed myself first, then by example I could perhaps have changed my family, and from their inspiration and encouragement to me I would have been better able to help my country and from there I may even have been able to change the world."*

Some of you reading this are hungry for your life to change. You don't like where you are in your marriage or your finances. You don't like where you are in relationship with your kids, your parents, your boyfriend, or your boss. You don't like where you are in your job. I have good news for you. **Followers of Jesus experience changed lives.** The testimony of every Christ follower is I once was this, now I am this. I once was lost, now I'm found. Once I was blind, now I can see. I once was a doubter, now I'm a believer. Something dramatic happens in the life of every Christ follower that makes them see differently, love differently, and live differently than they did before they met Jesus and began to follow Him.

Jesus was walking one day through the streets of the city of Jericho. A large crowd was following Him. There was a blind beggar by the side of the road whose name was Bartimaeus. If anyone needed a change in his life, it was Bartimaeus. Being blind in Jesus' day meant you couldn't work, and obviously you couldn't read or write. There were no Seeing Eye dogs; there weren't a lot of the amenities that we have today that help those who are blind. He was reduced to simply begging for living. Every day somebody would carry him out to the side of the road and set him on a pallet. He would beg for sustenance day after day. At the end of the day someone would take him back home. It was a miserable life. But one day everything changed when Jesus arrived in town.

Bartimaeus was so desperate for change that when he heard Jesus was close by, he shouted to the top of his lungs and begged for Jesus to help him. The people around him tried to calm him down and told him to be quiet. He shouted even louder, not caring what others thought. Bartimaeus does something that you and I must do if we ever intend to experience the ride of our lives. **He recognized the opportunity to change.** There was no way he was missing this. He took advantage of Jesus coming by his street corner that day. When Bartimaeus awoke that morning he had no idea that Jesus Christ would be passing by his spot near the road. As best as he knew it was just another ordinary day. He would be sitting at the same place, doing the same thing, living the same miserable lifestyle. There was no time to prepare for Jesus. It was just an opportunity that dropped into his lap. He needed to seize the moment. If you are in need of change in your life, you must seize the opportunity to change. The truth is, most of the time we already know the right things to do. Not only that, we know the benefits of doing the right things in life. However, we put it off and we never do it. Therefore, we miss the opportunity to change and we fail to experience the ride.

Among all the crowd noise, Jesus heard this man's voice. He walks over to a guy who's a blind beggar, sitting on the ground by the road and asks an interesting question, *"What would you like Me to do for you?"* Why in the world did Jesus ask this? He already knew what Bartimaeus' problem was. Why in the world would Jesus look at him and say, *"What do you want Me to do for you?"* Isn't it obvious? By asking that question Jesus allowed Bartimaeus to admit his need. **If we are ever to experience change, we need to admit the need for change.** We must come to the point where we admit the road we've been on isn't working out. It is necessary to acknowledge the road map we've been following isn't getting us where we need to be. Here's the amazing thing: Jesus Christ asks you the identical question today. *"What do you want Me to do for you?"* He desires to make changes in your life. He would like to do incredible things in your life. But you must admit that you need to change. Most people refuse to do this. Whether it's pride or fear or stubbornness or whatever, many people won't admit the need for change. Consequently, they never experience it and they wind up on a road that results in a destination where they never intended to go. You must admit your need for change if you ever want to experience a changed life. Bartimaeus recognized he had an opportunity for Jesus to change his life. When Jesus asked him what needed changing, Bartimaeus said *"I want to see. I don't want to beg anymore. I want to see so I can get a job and not depend on my friends and family to carry me to this street corner everyday. I want to see, Jesus, and from what I've heard, You're the only one who can change me. You're the only one who can heal me. Please, please change me."*

What happens next is amazing. The Bible says this man "received" his sight, which is an interesting word choice. It implies that he could have rejected the offer. He could have said *"You know what, Jesus? I've gotten used to this life of darkness and begging. Why change now? It's comfortable and I'm surviving. I'm making it; barely, but I'm making it."* He doesn't do that. This is his big opportunity for a changed life. What does he do? He accepts it. That's what you and I must do. **We need to receive the change**. God doesn't force us to change. He wants us to experience it but He won't force it on us. It can't be earned and you can't work for it. You certainly don't deserve it. It can't be gained by doing a bunch of religious rituals. You just receive the free gift of God's grace and the ability to change regardless of what your past has been. Some of you are carrying major conflict, major pain, major disappointment, and major grief in your life. Some of you are quite lonely and you feel that happiness has passed you by. You are to some extent like Bartimaeus sitting on the side of the road. You can put on a happy smile but inside you're hurting and in a lot of pain. You are begging for change and up to this point you are blind to the possibility that life could be different. Bartimaeus was blind, but he had enough vision to see that Jesus Christ could change him.

In closing this book I would like to reveal something within this narrative. The story begins with Bartimaeus sitting by the road side begging. That is his life before he meets Jesus. The story ends after he received his sight and the Bible says Bartimaeus followed Jesus along the road. One of those two phrases describes your life. You are either sitting beside the road needing a change in your life, or you are following Jesus because of the change in your life. Which one do you prefer to represent your life? Are you sitting by the road or following Jesus on the road?

Followers of Jesus experience changed lives. If you are not a Christ follower, my prayer is that I have persuaded you it is worth considering. My purpose has been to show you that it is not an endless, mindless game of "Copy Jesus". It is a far cry from imitating a God whose infinite holiness we will never equal. Instead, it is a relationship with the God who loves you. It is a connection that is life changing and leads to meaning and purpose. The ride begins by crossing the line of faith and asking Jesus to change your life. He will forgive your past; give meaning and purpose to the present; offer hope for a future of spending eternity with Him. Don't miss the joy of the ride of your life.

If you are already a Christ follower, and you are in need of change in a particular area of your life, I encourage you to begin following Jesus in that particular area. Whether it's your dating life, your marriage, your finances, your career, or whatever, change directions and begin to follow Jesus. Now is your opportunity to change. Admit your need for change. Receive the change Christ offers and follow Him down the road to your next destination. You will never regret it and as a result of following Jesus, you will experience the ride of your life.

CPSIA information can be obtained at www.ICGtesting.com
Printed in the USA
LVOW050514190712

290645LV00001B/33/P